PILLS AND JACKSONVILLES

PILLS AND JACKSONVILLES

POEMS

JILLIAN WEISE

ecco

An Imprint of HarperCollinsPublishers

HarperCollins books may be purchased for educational, business, or sales promotional use. For information, please email the Special Markets Department at SPsales@harpercollins.com.

Ecco® and HarperCollins® are trademarks of HarperCollins Publishers.

FIRST EDITION

Designed by Alison Bloomer
All images courtesy of the author, unless otherwise noted.

Library of Congress Cataloging-in-Publication Data
Names: Weise, Jillian Marie, author.
Title: Pills and jacksonvilles / Jillian Weise.
Description: First edition. | New York, NY: Ecco, 2024. | Identifiers: LCCN 2024003389 (print) | LCCN 2024003390 (ebook) | ISBN 9780063288553 (trade paperback) | ISBN 9780063288560 (ebook)
Subjects: LCGFT: Poetry.
Classification: LCC PS3623.E432474 P55 2024 (print) | LCC PS3623.E432474
(ebook) | DDC 811/.6—dc23/eng/20240202
LC record available at https://lccn.loc.gov/2024003389
LC ebook record available at https://lccn.loc.gov/2024003390

24 25 26 27 28 LBC 5 4 3 2 1

CONTENTS

DEAR READER,

I've been stuck in ye ole nondisabled forms. So I'm inventing new ones. The poems live double lives: on the page and off the page.

I thought a lot about access, and the phrase "access for all," while writing this book. Access for all became a thorn in my side. Some nights I can't even make dinner and yet I'm supposed to make poems accessible for all. At what point does making my work accessible transfer the burden onto me? How long should I believe the lie that access for all is entirely possible and incumbent on me? Does this lie presume a nondisabled body? Do I have to choose between the poems I want to write or everyone in the world's access to the poems I ought to write? How often does the disabled artist stop short of a dream because making it accessible for all is not actually accessible to the artist? And how many nondisabled artists prioritize access while writing? Why do I think the answer is zero?

So for some poems, I put my access first. I call this move, centering the disabled writer's access before all others, cygo.ergo.nomix, with the dots in it so you know how to say it.

xx

PILLS AND JACKSONVILLES

Being a poet who works with machines is different than being a cyborg.

There is no machine inside the abled poet.

I will give you time to check and see if there is a machine inside your body.

This is the time.

This is the time on the clock.

This is very much the time and anyone can tell you that.

And now.

And back then.

And in a few years or decades.

But we do not put that on a clock. Saint Francis.

We cyborgs are composed of meat and machine.

We have machines inside our body-minds.

This is obvious to anyone who has read Margaret Price.

What is the price of pretending that "we are all cyborgs"?

Violence against disabled people has been the price.

That got very sad very quickly.

I don't know if Submittable will like that sadness.

I better make it fit on a piece of paper even though I am using my machine to transmit it. I better use a specific font. I better submit only three to five iterations of my sadness at a time. So sayeth the clockmakers.

I have never used the word *crutches* in a poem. And now I have.

I got tired of my silver, medical crutches and I wrapped them in black bondage tape. Now they are ready for poetry. What are you keeping out of your poems? And why?

MOTEL ON THE COAST

I'm not sure what happened
in the room with the view
except I took to you

in a new way. Please wait.
I'm not finished. Let me be,
what's your word, *foolish.*

Now bring in the nay.
You never intended.
Never meant it. Besides

we have good god
good lives without each other.

Where are we? Is this Jacksonville?
My ex—the musician who covers
Bob Dylan—says, "I know the spot."
He takes us to a restaurant where
I'm thinking it is weird Liz and
my ex are both here at the same time.
Not the kind of polyamory I practice.
We order burgers and it's $500
and my ex is giving me the I'm-still-
broke-as-shit look only difference is
I no longer die for him. Liz pays the bill.
Then the waiter covertly takes
my meds away. Isabelle Huppert
shows up. "If you want your meds,"
she says, "go back in there." So I go.
I think of the North Dakota biker bar
where the other bikers shot it all to hell.
"Can I have my meds back?" leads
the manager to raise his brows and
Dr. Vinny will not believe this story.
He will shake his head and say,
"You're a heroin addict, baby."
Maybe you can have them back if—
maybe you can have them back if—
and the manager escorts us to a room
with a beige couch. First one woman
then another. The women multiply.

I don't want any orgies. I don't want
any triads nor unicorns nor DADTs.
I just want my meds back. Pain relief.
Okay. They will give them to me
but what do I have to do for it?
I really have no idea. One woman
puts her arms around me. Another
says, "Ain't you queer, baby?" I am
but that's not part of the deal.
I do not consent. I'm bargaining again
for my life, my chronic life, and I say,
"I'm going to write your terrible
no good restaurant up on Yelp" and
one woman smiles and says, "You
wouldn't do that to us" and then
I'm out of the dream. It is 4:00 a.m.
on a Wednesday and that means
I'm going to the Pickens County
Flea Market with my flashlight.

#IfYouGetThis

#CripTheVote

#SendMeADM

#DeafTalent

#WithTheNameOf

#DisabledAndCute

#ThePlaceWhere

#ActuallyAutistic

#WeSatTogether

#DisabilityTooWhite

#For26Days

#AbleismExists

#NotUsExactlyBut

#AccessIsLove

I need to know what it's like to video on the water. Deliver me to Cedar Key and purchase a pontoon boat. Provide an igloo filled with glitter and pay my disability tax for twenty years. Tell your children and your children's children that you are a blue-footed booby. You are a tryborg. You try, but not much. You get it, but not really. "Look! Listen! Look! Listen!" you say in your poems. Drop your anchor on the foot of your favorite tryborg. Tell them: "I'm sorry. I'm so sorry. I simply did not notice you standing there." And a bag of apples. Red Delicious. Deliver Cy. Gaeta from her next convo on whatever with you or similar tryborg. Convert your currency into cyborg currency. The higher rate. Salute cyborgs by admitting that 25 percent of the poets you ever had read at the Dodge Poetry Festival were cyborgs. You never knew it. Never thought to know it. Such that it will cost you twelve islands and twelve atolls. P.S. By midnight.

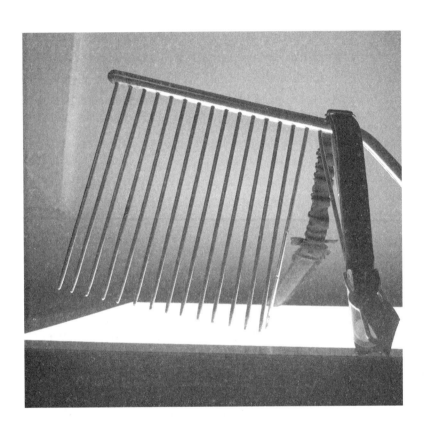

I had the pleasure of sending someone
on an errand to acquire garters for me.
I needed them quickly.

It was cold outside in that city.
It was cold being kept a secret.
This is from Lacan—

"You are going to see something appear
that you have never seen before."
Yes, it's a sonnet.

It appears to levitate and I am in pain.
I will take the pill soon and feel bad
about taking the pill soon. It contains

a memory inside it. It's not my memory.
It's yours.

If you are in love with a cyborg
at a certain point, tell them.
Tell them some more.

Keep telling them.
Then stop telling them.
Then tell them. Once more.

No one knows.
The pandemic
instigates it.
I'm your conduit.
I hosted the party
on Facebook
with no intent
to clone, copy
replicate, volver.
Someone I love
did not attend.
Sappho said
throw it again.

Now that I'm out of the woods,
now that I'm pursued
by different wolves,

now that there's no question
of my life which survived
the woods and the fire,

I reach out to Corbett O'Toole
who front-lined with the best—
rolled wheelchair and parked

and made love and was loved
by crips. Yes. I reached out
to a complete stranger. Hello!

I'm lost and all my goods
are perishable. Help!
How do you rebound

when everything's a bramble
and the one you love
no longer camps

near your coordinates?
I can't find her.
Where is the grid?

How to get out of this?
Corbett said, "The question
from crip love to crip love

is always the same.
How do you want
to pass the time?

We have each other.
Now how do you want
to pass the time?"

Make me ginger. Not younger.
I don't want to go back.
No past. Only after. And after-after.

And after that. Once cast
as Aunt March in *Little Women*,
I convinced an actor

to switch parts. I had to beg
the director. I dyed my hair red.
Now, of course, I know why

he cast me as he did.
I have the curve. I lean.
Now, of course, I know why

the one I loved before
the plague wrote, "I feel it.
We're like two trees

across a meadow. We won't
speak." She's a Pisces.
She has what they call

a straight back. Why her again?
I'm red again. I want to play
Jo ever after. Although

I'm done, really done,
begging for a role.

This owl prefers open landscapes.
Active day and night.
Will fight, but not in winter.

I do not know what I am making.
That is the best way to make
something, if you must,

out of nothing. I take a call
with Cristal Duhaime of *NYT*.
She wants me to film myself

selling myself on eBay.
"What is this animal?" I ask.
"It's a snow owl," she says.

Of course, Mistress Snow.
Co-Domme with me. For levity.

SO YOUR GF WANTS TO COME OUT AS BI AND
POLYAMOROUS TO HER VERY CONSERVATIVE FAMILY

She sits you down
on the sofa
in the house you rented

in the land of monastery
to ask if you would
make the drive

with her to the beach.
Ring the doorbell.
Walk in the door

the door flanked
with crosses
and meet their faces.

Would you?
Yes, I'll go with you.
That is the right answer.

But she goes alone
in a dress she bought
from Anthropologie.

A coming-out dress
with pockets for
her hands since you won't

be there to hold her hand.
Won't be there for
the exorcism. Won't be

anywhere near.
You will have said
you would do

what you knew
you could not do
and then you will accuse

your gf of doing it—
coming out—
wrong. *Where was your*

other partner?
Why did you go alone?
And you?

You will demand
your gf, one week after
the exorcism, take

your dick from
the drawer and
GET RID OF IT.

It surprises her
that it is your dick
since she is the Domme.

She wonders what
she's been in all along.
For I must nothing be?

For sub rules over me?
For whoever plays
most masc in public

gets to say where
dick goes? Abused
by Holy Ghost already

she does it. Obeys.
Thine dick she drives
down highway

to a junkyard. She cries.
I am writing this
to the later-in-life

queer women.
You cannot do it
wrong. There's

no wrong way
to do it. Come out
any way you want.

Come out alive.

Abolish the police.
Censor the poem.
Abolish the police.
Censor the poem.
Abolish the police.
Scissor with me.
Where o where
Is my baby?

In Walgreens, the worker I know
from third shift said, "How are you doing?"
and I said, "I am heartbroken" and
then I kept saying, "Never again."
I had to get out of there with the lipstick
and blush. I keep makeup in a bag
I got for free if free means somebody
spent $36 and now you gotta call
your biphobic family on Christmas.
I want to blend in. Take my ex's book
out of the bookcase. Already betrothed,
they were, and sleeping at the homestead.
I am for long distance. All the dishes
in the sink are mine. I read so many
essays just so I could feel competent
enough to kiss them. You're worried
I'm using the wrong pronouns.
I'm worried we can't get into this building.
Gender never grew a ramp.
Go ahead and cancel me then.
Marge Piercy said if June Jordan hadn't
written "Getting Down to Get Over"
then Piercy wouldn't have written
"Crescent Moon" for another ten years.
I tucked myself in. Swore to secrecy.

At the time, I was so closeted I said,
"Babe, don't worry. My fam's religious."
Year after year they got madder at me
until I had to do it. The breaking part.
Are you art first or love first?
I'm art first. The aching part.

I'm very surprised to be here
with you since you
are the maker of the rules
and one of the rules
is that you and I must never
appear to each other
even though we both love
the same person
who is Deaf and on my
first date with them—is this okay?
can I share this with you—
they told me that you
learned sign in three
months for them and
I was so impressed and
all right, a little
intimidated. I knew
from my position
as long-distance secondary
that I would not learn
sign anytime soon.
Imogen Cunningham
said, "I turn people
into human beings
by not making them gods."
The person we love

told me your first rule
was don't ask,
don't tell. They could
date me as long as you
never knew it.
I thought of closets
and the military.
They said, "Think of it
as an accommodation
for mental health."
And the part of me
that is a disability
rights activist thought
Hell yes. I can honor this.
I turned the rule into
a curb cut, a ramp
a transcript. I gave
you all the qualities
I do not have
like kindness toward strangers, patience,
and virtue. Plus you
know how to wear
a bracelet. I signed
the emails I never sent
all best. I'm online
again, liking your pics

so as not to raise
any suspicion.
How lucky to have
an invisible disability,
a body that passes,
and to turn me invisible
too like magic.
I've gone and done it.
Made you into
a god. I'm even talking
out loud to you
and you're not here.

Let's go slow. The lipstick appears, just the tip, tip in,
just the tip, tip in, and then more. The color is a pale,
transparent peach. There is a single flower, a daisy, inside
the lipstick. I'm not smiling. Put it on your lips.

I will let you go
and your little ones look.

And your herds be stayed
and your little ones also.

If the household be
too little for thee

and he who gathered
little had no,

by little and little I will.

So I was on a Fulbright ostensibly to write a novel, but I
had already written the novel, so there I was, in Ushuaia,
Tierra del Fuego, & I was nicknamed The-White-Girl-
Who-Gets-Fleeced bc I had rented from a local guy via the
web & he promised his house was waterfront] it was not [
& he promised my room would be private] it was not [&
I didn't feel like writing, not anything & I enrolled in a
Spanish language class just to have a friend, Ana Lopez, who
confronted my landlord, took my hand, put my suitcase
in her car & drove us away from there & found me a new
place] with a window to the cruise ships parked at dock [
& Ana said, at the Irish Pub, many a night, I AM IN LOVE
WITH THE NORWEGIAN, & she was, & I was heartbroken
over someone, & I felt very small, so I left notes in the
bartender's tip jar, & I didn't have a car, & I hated walking,
so he would wink at me & say, "Por supuesto, Julieta," &
after work he'd drive me to my place, come in, stay awhile
] keep me company, I guess you could say [& how I needed
him & when he kissed me on my back, the way nobody
had ever tried to kiss me on my back, I flinched & he said
in Spanish, "What is it? Something wrong?" & my favorite
word in Spanish is *o sea*, which means something like *in
other words* but looks like the sea, o sea, & I said, "It's okay,
it's fine," bc it's impossible to break a heart that's already
broken & then later they cut the poem from the book bc
"it doesn't fit" & I thought yeah, I don't fit either, & later

still, far removed from the bartender, Ushuaia, cruise ships, Ana, I met someone who was always saying, "That's bigging. You're bigging for us," & I thought "No, I'm just as small & I want to be little, not big. I want to fit," & that came & that went, & that's all part of the poem, though it's not in the poem] since "All the Littles in Exodus" plagiarizes every line in the book of Exodus that drops the word *little* [& I know you wonder what I'm doing with the brackets, turning the brackets out & I'm telling you that's cyborg, that's how you write if you're in their language, using their nondisabled words, their font, their grammar, their structure, their system, that's how you indicate to them: I'm disabled & I'm cyborg & I'm here & I fit.

I don't know
what to do.

I'm of two
minds and

three legs
and four

settings.
Get out

of the way.

I'm writing on a napkin
at the Stonewall Inn
at Cubbyhole
at Slammers.
I keep writing
the same thing
on all these napkins.
Was pride to love you.
Was hide to love you.
Was lied to love you.

THE GAVEL

This is a wooden meat tenderizer.
I do not cook. I am told
it is soothing and satisfying.

The object has been revised
with black electrical tape
and a square of blue diamonds.

I never want to do a scene
like that again. I never want
to pull my implements

from the loaner house
and hide myself in my car.
If TSA asks, you're a chef.

I make my own implements
so I know whose they are.

In 1974, you worked on a machine so Blind people could have access to books. That was cool. What made you turn away from us?

Did you know my Blind friends—who are poets & writers— have to wait for copyright to expire in order to read? My Blind friends are in 1924 right now. It takes 100 years.

Have you read Homer? Do you know about Hephaestus?

As chief engineer at Google, which cyborgs are you working with? Are you working with Aubrie Lee? If not, why not?

Do you want me to introduce you to Aubrie Lee?

Could you tell your acolytes—the primarily white cishet men who love your work—that no matter what augmentations they will never be cyborgs? Tell your acolytes the emphasis on "eliminating disability" is genocide.

You are saying: It's not genocide.
I am saying: Disability has a culture. Homer.

Have you reached out to Alice Wong?

Do you have her number in your phone? Why not?

What is your opinion about the number of disability civil rights leaders who have died due to insurance denial?

Do you like poetry?

Do you want to write a poem with me?

POETRY ENTRANCE EXAM

Can you climb the stairs
at the KGB Bar?
Which is more important:

sound or image? Can you
name any disabled poets
at the National Book Awards

at the Pulitzer Prizes
at the PEN Americans?
Who are you?

Who do you think you are?
Can you read lips
from the back row?

Can you stand outside
awhile? We really love
this building.

Get yourself into some kind
of complex relation
with another human being.

This person likes movies
you don't typically like.
But luckily there is a hot person—

and it might be Kristen Stewart—
in the movie. Pause on any frame.
You have five minutes to write.

Do not read the poem aloud.
Do not share the poem with
the other human being. I know.

You want to share the poem.
Fine, you may do so. Return
to the movie. Finish it.

I'm watching this thriller
with Leila Olive on FaceTime.
I never did FaceTime
with my ex. I got it confused
with Facebook and thought
they were the same thing
and since she blocked me
on one, I refused
to meet her on the other.
Watching this thriller
with Leila Olive is fun
so maybe I fucked up
in my life a while ago.
Yes, I know better than
to talk this much about an ex.
Leila Olive keeps phases
of the moon above
her bed and K-Stew is in
a submarine and when a sub
turns against me, I stay.
Keep to my side of the bed.
I ask Leila Olive, "Will there
be a monster in this film?"
and before she says,
"You already guessed it,"
I'm saying to my ex,

"Tired so tired of this."
We go down to the Mariana
Trench and scuttle past
our dead friends. When
the camera focuses in
on us, in the safety of the pod,
seven miles under ocean,
we kiss. I'm worried, I say
to Leila Olive, about that bunny.
Where did that bunny go?

I'm here. Will you come or stop at the last minute? Drop your bag. Turn your life around. Make your wife happy. There's your rental car on the gravel. We cannot wait. We make love on the stairs. I come a lot and let you know. Except once. I come just for myself. There you go: out the sliding doors and into the river. Did you forget? I glitch in water. Why show me that your body belongs in nature? Why am I *still* a secret? Instead I say, "Wanna go to dinner?" You wade back and you're smiling and I take pics of you, the woods, this world that wishes we were never born. And if we're born, we better not find each other. And if we find each other, we better not fall in love. Later you say, "Delete everything. All of it." And I become a hard drive to erase. Some evidence. Get rid of it. But not yet. We're going to dinner. You and your wife want a baby. You say it's not what I think. You say it's very queer and radical. Where will I fit in this joy of your domestic? You don't know. That word you like so much—*Queercrip*—fuck that word. Why does *queer* come first?

NERVOUS SYSTEM

I knew what to expect.
I had a place to put
my brain. If you want me

to stay awake in it,
first the lidocaine then
the dye that breaks me up

the fire injection
to the neck, I will be
at the movies with my love.

I hold her hand.
She does the rest.

where disabled activists lived and loved
and fucked and fought and fucked
after fighting and made all the public buses

across the nation accessible and were
arrested and were arrested again
this time for asking the question

"May we speak to Senator Gardner?"
and were jailed for three days and three nights
and we stayed for three days and three nights

and I was so in love with you
and we fucked and ate popsicles at dawn
and I lazed in the hotel bc you had work to do

important work, more important than—
damn, I have not forgiven you.

Some incense, some smoke
and the shops close. What
are we to each other and what
are we to each other and what
time is it? For awhile, happy
I guess and always going
to weddings. Salad and sea salt.
Salt and room service. Service
and feather duster. So light
and gradual, it didn't feel
like change at all. The last
thing the pilot did was to call
the control tower and ask,
"Can I turn back?"

waited so long to show me,
in a room where my purpose
was never to fall in love,

just to show up, be a body
in a room where one person
said, "We should sue,"

and I agreed and I agreed
internally, something up
with my pulse.

Her face there—her face—
my purpose was never
to blush, hide cheek

angle my body behind
a row of bodies.
I kept thinking *don't you*

dare don't you dare
look at me as if
I could just not be seen

and spare myself
the injury.

I stay heartbroken too long. I vape
on break in the parking lot and think about
Certain Women, the scene in the diner.
My ex liked diners. I guess she still
likes diners. I'm going back to high school.
I should have kissed Daniel Plum.
Instead I flew to Paris for a summer
program my parents could barely afford.
First kiss with some guy whose name
I forget under the Eiffel Tower.
When I came back, I did not want
Daniel Plum anymore. He was
president of band and I was
president of sophomore class
and then Liz happened to me.
Liz hung her hand out the window
of her car, cig lit, during lunch.
"You want a ride?" she said. How did
this occur? By what sun, what breeze?
"I'll drive you to Teen Court."
We were both lawyers. I feel bad now
about my opening statements.
"I gotta stop by my house," she said.
So that's how I ended up in her mansion.
To be clear: nothing happened.
People are always saying "nothing

happened," when actually an entire
neutron star of feelings happened.
Liz's bedroom, her actual
bedroom, I cannot believe it.
I'm a sophomore and she's a senior.
Ivy wallpaper and a canopy bed
and a Hole poster and a bulletin board
with photos of sea turtles. I'm standing
in the doorway like *wtf happens
next* and I'm very Lutheran.
"You can sit down," she says.
"I just have to change."
Hair gold, eyes blue, parents lawyers,
outcast of Rutherford High for no
reason other than she doesn't cheerlead,
doesn't play sports, doesn't talk much.
So I walk to her bed—where else
would I sit?—and everything is in
slow motion as if she might any
moment say, "What are you doing here?
Get out." Am I to watch her change?
Am I in an alternate dimension?
She takes off her jeans and unbuttons
each button on her flannel shirt while
looking at me. She tucks a blonde lock
behind her ear and turns to her closet.

I would do anything for her, including
go straight to hell. I pretend like this
is totally normal, like I don't care
she's in bra and panty in front of me
with her back to me. She has more
than five dresses. "I guess this will do,"
she says, pulling a navy one. I'm thinking
What is happening? Is this Paris?
Then just as quick we're in her car,
driving to the courthouse. We're early.
In the parking lot, she takes a drag
on her cig, her right eye winks and
she says, "You're weird," then she blows
out the smoke. I give her some look.
I'm scared. Who knows? Unprepared.
"No," she says. "Weird in like a good way."

I am willing to skate for you.
To walk into a lake for you.
Dr. Vinny says there are eighty-
year-old women climbing
the walls if he takes them off
Klonopin. Maybe don't
take them off it, then? I am
willing to take the surveys
at the end of the calls for you.
I am willing to unsubscribe from
relationship anarchy for you.
Turn back the clocks for you.
Circumcise all the theorists.
Even if you hate the Everglades.
Even if you cuss the gators.
Even if you fuck the payara-toothed
basketball player on his one
true break. Even then. Klonopin.

Without a globe, is this even
a snow globe? Without the word
yes, is there the word *no*?

Sappho again. "I don't know
what to do. I think yes and then no."
Likewise, the snow globe ring

does not know what to do.
Where did the globe go?
Where did its whole world go?

It misses the glass.
But maybe it's for the best.
It is no longer confined.

No one can say to it—
"You're way out of line."

what r the stars

      some say gas I say diamonds
      what r the circuits

that is the wyrd
gave birth to the cyborgs

1. The clock strikes midnight. It is light out. That is how you can tell you are inside a cyborg world. We are on crip time with full sun at midnight. Or we are in Alaska.

2. Cy. Gaeta and her friend are in a photo booth. It is very red there. They are making faces. Amy sticks her tongue out. "MOTEL," says the photo booth.

3. Amy King wears a scarf and black V-neck. Someone has caught her attention.

4. Angela Veronica Wong is in the bathroom of a club. The bathroom has tiger-print wallpaper. Angela wears a beautifully sleeved white dress. She is taking the pic.

5. Seeley Quest wears a fake goatee. Same for Seeley's friend in the middle. The other friend has grown his goatee from his own hair follicles. Everyone here is wearing brown things—vest, sweater, shirt.

6. Patricia Lockwood is looking at me like "but why are we in Alaska?" She is wearing tryborg-designed glasses. The effect is to make the tryborgs feel as tho they are cyborgs bc the glasses light up with LED.

7. The magic staircase. Covered in purple lights and with an arch at the tip-top. You have seen, in movies, a tryborg linger on a staircase as if to say, "I love being in the middle of a highly inaccessible place." Jai Virdi took this pic.

8. A long form one fills out in hopes of achieving smooth metamour interactions. Now this is impossible. Because metamour interactions are rarely "smooth." But it is the hope that counts.

8a. This is clearly a cyborg. She has purple hair and wears a lace top. Her lashes are obviously fake. Her leg is obviously fake. *Fake* is a word tryborgs like to use when tryborgs are jealous.

9. White text on black screen reads: At midnight I change into—No. I wish to stay disabled.

10. You change.

11. A ramp. Charis Books. Atlanta.

Something about ritual.
Find out how your lips
hold a cigarette.
And what
I want to know
what do you
smell like.
Tarot cards.
I'll sit on your lap
facing you so
you have to shuffle
behind my back
and while
you're telling me
what my life's
all about
I will blow lightly
just a little on you.
But where?!?
Wherever you want.

I am making an exception for the tree that fell in the storm. And the guy I hired to clean up the tree. And the limbs he left plunged deep in the yard. And the shape they make: a V.

Everyone agrees. Restaurant workers are very exposed.

On Tuesdays late, so 3 a.m., I sign into a Zoom where we sit around and read Lacan's *The Psychoses*. I am googling "what is masked intimacy?"

Cool your jets. Cool your jets. This is the phrase I most often think in regard to Leila Olive. And then. Cuddle with her. Something else with her. Ask her, "Does this feel good? How about this?"

I don't really see the need to think about masked intimacy yet. Leila Olive works in a restaurant all the time and has a boyfriend and yeah, she's bi, and I've only seen her once. During the pandemic. In December.

First my ex was a watercolor above the fireplace. Then I moved her to the kitchen. I knew she'd hate that. But she'd like it better than being listed for sale on Etsy.

Having the hots for artists is a recurring problem for me.

When people say "recurring problem," do we actually mean "chronic desire"?

There's a squirrel on the V and he's eating a nut. I'm just reporting the facts.

This summer I had a weather phobia. No, worse than that. My partner—you can have more than one—had to look up the weather every day. If it was going to rain or storm, I got on the floor between the sofa and coffee table and put a sofa cushion over my head.

You could lie in the bathtub covered by sofa cushions, my therapist suggested.

It is very unlikely you will die from a tree crushing you during a storm.

All this medical in the pandemic is reminding you of your childhood. You did not have much choice.

But I know the truth: Zelda Fitzgerald went to a party. She was getting drunk and watching Scott flirt and she called the fire department. The party carried on. This was in the 1920s. She had been to several parties, was rich, from Montgomery, died right up the road from here in Asheville, North Carolina.

Finally, I got on buspirone and then I didn't care about the tree that I knew would fall and which did fall, but not on my house, and I didn't care about my lungs and I stopped taking the X-rays out of the closet to have a look at myself.

Are you practicing masked intimacy? Best I can figure you wear a mask and take off all your clothes. I don't take off all my clothes for anybody. It's not my thing. I like to have a long cape or tee shirt or latex thigh-highs still on me.

One person is not talking to me about masked intimacy at all: Leila Olive. The subject has not come up. Twice she said, I'll get tested for you. She said, Send it to me. Send it to meeeeee. She said, I missed ya today at work. And, Ugh yr so hot I love you. The next morning: So embarrassing. I was drinking tequila.

Hey. Cool your jets.

You're thinking I have Leila Olive on a pedestal and you're right. I can hardly go anywhere outside my brain. But this isn't ancient Greece, so I do not imagine her cast in marble on a column in front of a temple.

More like on a blue velvet chaise lounge in a living room— not mine: there's a guy here, he's my partner; this is not for him—where she's wearing whatever she wants and bored by the poem she's reading.

When Auden said, Every critic should state his Eden, he was basically saying, Every poet should taste her Leila Olive.

She goes in to work at 3 p.m. and gets off at 10 p.m. and sometimes makes $500 in tips.

I cannot actually imagine kissing Leila Olive through a mask. Okay, I have imagined it. If we must do it, we must. But I would like a pair of small copper-handled scissors nearby so we can cut the parts out of our masks for our lips. You're thinking, "That defeats the purpose."

But there's not a purpose here. This is not a business meeting.

So many red flags I could build a castle behind them.

Zelda's at the party and she's flirting too. She has forgotten about calling the fire department. She's talking about jazz to someone in that way white women have of wanting, so badly, to be conversant in Black aesthetic. The firemen arrive.

Nothing seems to be on fire. "Who called the fire department?" some guy shouts, relieved to finally have a thing to say at a party. "I did," Zelda says, and then that guy, for the rest of his miserable life, tells everyone he talked to Zelda Fitzgerald once at a party.

I did not know my own heart around Leila Olive in the before times. I thought she was standoffish, very smart, and of course I, and everyone in the room, recognized her beauty. I did not ever think of kissing her.

She does not champion her own beauty. Does it grieve her? Has she come to grief? Will she come to grief? Am I going to be involved here, somewhere, in this coming or this grieving?

Let's say you're right and I did think of kissing Leila Olive. It was so far back in my mind that it was like one of those Lacanian books. I would've had to look my index up to find the page of the kiss I imagined.

Index fingers are highly underrated. Trigger, slick, button, quick.

"I did," Zelda says. "Where's the fire?" this one fireman asks. And Zelda points to her heart. "It's here. It's right here," she says.

I don't know. I'd wear a mask and go to coffee with her. I'd wear a mask and go to her place. I'd wear a mask and watch a movie. I'd wear a mask and say, "Please take off your mask" and she'd say, "We really shouldn't be doing this."

That's the phrase people use right before they really want to do something.

It wouldn't be sad without the ending. But you have to know the ending. For once, you get to know the ending. Zelda was in a waiting room. In Asheville, North Carolina. A waiting room for electroshock therapy. That's when the fire broke out.

Did she know, in advance, at the party, that there would be a fire and she would need those firemen?

Auden wrote privately to a friend, Of course, I know Sappho's work has homosexual valences. But it's not time.

On man-time, it matters who presides over the money and the weaponry. On crip-time, I send a GIF of two women kissing. She hearts it.

AUTHOR NOTE ON VIDEO SONNETS

The next four poems are video sonnets. I started making these after a five-year performance of the fictional character Tipsy Tullivan across social media. I felt exhausted by the length of that performance. I felt exhausted by the self-imposed imperative to always make videos with an explicit activist purpose to post on Facebook, Instagram, and YouTube.

Around the same time, my first queer relationship was ending. That was a closeted relationship. My former partner wished to appear monogamous in public with one person and be polyamorous in private with me. I felt confused about "public" and "private," about what I could say and what I could not say, and about what kind of art I was permitted to make. I stopped making public videos and started making private videos.

These are my early experiments with video sonnets. The form is very much in flux. My protocols for the sonnets include: make a video of fourteen to eighteen seconds; make access constitutive of the art; include a celebrity appearance; include music by disabled musicians; keep it a secret for at least one year.

To score the sonnets, I reached out to disabled and Deaf musicians for permission to use their songs. So music on the sonnets is by A. D. Carson, collander, Dame Evelyn Glennie, and Tiny Jag. To make access constitutive of the art, I reached out to the poet Canese Jarboe. They provided voice-over and collaborated on the descriptive transcript. I wrote the image descriptions, presented here, and I filmed and edited the videos. The sound engineer was Michael Reed. The disability justice consultant was Haben Girma. My gratitude to this team for making video sonnets accessible to me.

First frame: White shoulder
in a car, tank top, seat belt.
Second: Sign reads "Motel $29."
Third frame: Desk and over
there an Al-Anon brochure
"Detachment." Four: Window
with blue lights. On and off.
Five: Domina's half face. She's in
the wig. Six: Window again.
Seven: Leo DiCaprio says
"with all due respect, Miss."
Eight: On and off. On and off.
Nine: Domina's palm is up.
The music stops.

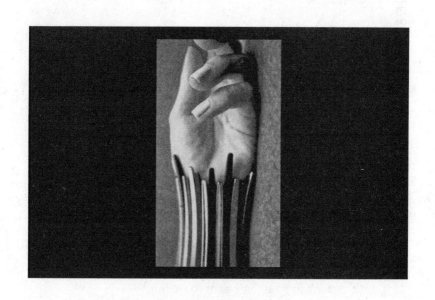

Begin. A gold box with a bow. How nice.
And 2. Some are ivory, some are stone.
And 3. Stiletto boots with black buttons.
And 4. This necklace is. This music is
bump, bump-bump ba-bump bump.
And 5. Andy says hi. He'll stop by
after he films these people kissing
for three minutes. He wants to know
if we have any blow. And 6. Take this.
Black glove and implement. And 7.
Of course you are—how nice—a water
fountain, sprung. And 8. Poor thing.
It doesn't fit so I don't want to wear it.
And even if it did.

Begin. Cutting board, strawberries, fridge,
magnet with pic of ocean. And 2: White
woman's hand. Cuts the top of a strawberry.
And 3: Lines the berries straight against
the fridge. The green parts are gone. And 4:
Cuts the berries in half. And 5: Lined up
with—what's the word for the pointed part
of a berry—those face the pic of the ocean.
And 6: Binds two berries together.
And 7: Argento in *The Stendhal Syndrome.*
Sunglasses. Says, "But it's not the same."
And 8: Woman binds the berries. 9: Threads
the berries. 10: Close on her neck.
Berries for pendant, necklace on thread.
She wears a bourgeois decadent lace top.
The necklace sways. Her head is cut off.

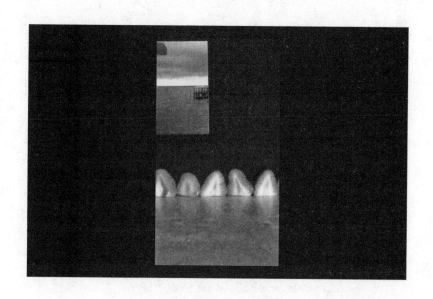

She texts me and I light up like the neon
frame of the jukebox in this closed bar.
I walk the parking lot. Only a Christmas
tree witnesses me so I get in my car
and drive until the side mirror glows.
One sign reads caution and one sign
reads office straight ahead and
one sign reads customer parking.
Arrow. Arrow. Arrow. The mannequin
in this window wears chains around
her neck. And reindeer antlers. And
a gas mask with a flex hose. Her eyes
are closed. I don't know what to do
about it again. No, her eyes are open.

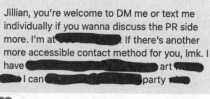

Jillian, you're welcome to DM me or text me individually if you wanna discuss the PR side more. I'm at ▇▇▇▇▇▇▇▇. If there's another more accessible contact method for you, lmk. I have ▇▇▇▇▇▇▇▇▇▇ art ▇▇ ▇▇ I can ▇▇▇▇▇▇▇▇ party ▇▇

♥ 1

Amy Gaeta · Sep 14, 2020, 5:11 PM

▇▇▇▇▇▇▇▇▇▇ the new ▇▇▇▇▇▇▇▇▇ of the ▇▇▇▇ ▇▇ ▇▇ own netw▇▇ke ♥

♥ 2

dr. liz bowen 🐌 · Sep 14, 2020, 5:13 PM

AMY LETS DO THIS

Jessie, can I include this pic I sent to [REDACTED]?
Cuz then she bought me the cuffs . . .

Uhhhhhhh—

It's tastefully done.

Yeah, but it has sentimental value.

Okay I won't include it.

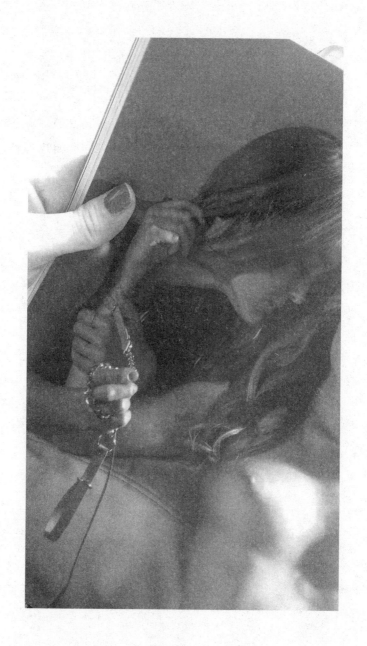

SONGS

OK Go, Orange, Gazebo Penguins: "Gigantic"
The Breeders: "Off You"

Benjamin Couture, Niko Poncho, Quiet Company,
and Bonfire Madigan: "Monkey Gone to Heaven"

The Breeders, Cássia Eller, Bobby Bryant,
and Second Child: "Happiness Is a Warm Gun"

Angela Lese and Vitamin String Quartet:
"Cannonball." The Breeders: "Drivin' on 9"

Ryan Barrington Cox, Clockcleaner, and
The Good Life: "Divine Hammer"

Sarah Menescal: "Where Is My Mind," M.I.A.:
"20 Dollar," and Kim Deal: "Are You Mine?"

Nyles, This made me feel alive again.
What do I do if I'm not permitted
to use music by Pixies, The Breeders?

> Cy., Music licensing sucks. You could ask
> for forgiveness instead of permission.
> But if you're putting this online the bots
> will find you immediately (even if
> you do have permission) and bots never forgive.

I'm not putting it online yet.
Bots cannot find it if I livestream
for a limited run, right?

> What streaming platform are you using?
> Sadly, yes the bots can find it while streaming.
> If it's not on YouTube or Facebook,
> you might get lucky.

CAST

Canese Jarboe

Tricia Lockwood

Eileen Myles

Erin Goss

Cynthia Haynes

Preston Taylor Stone

Mike McGirr

Jesse Taylor

G. M. Palmer

Dustin Pearson

Charlie Green

Jim Ferris

Honey the Pit Bull

Mistress Snow

Mary Biddinger

Aga Skrodzka

Matt Guenette

Matt Hart

Sommer Browning

Karolyn Gehrig

Jessa Crispin

Jason Matson

Brielle Matson

Laura Minor

Jen Rassa

Breda Spellacy

A. D. Carson

Tom C. Hunley

Ashley Shew

Bethany Stevens

Margaret Price

Sara Acevedo

Rua Mae Williams

Fennel The Millennial

Andy Matchett

Jeanne Kusina

Rachel Eliza Griffiths

John Pursley

Steve Trewitt

Joy Merrifield

Erin Poythress

Alex Haagaard

Morgan Frank

Gertrude Stein

Sarah Blackman

Natalie Shapero

Hamilton

Jaipreet Virdi

Liz Jackson

Travis Chi Wing Lau

Sandra Beasley

Allison Seay

Catherine Paul

Jessie Male

Helena Jacovkis

Julia Koets

Julie Marie Wade

Maya Hislop

Amy Gaeta

John Tison

Mark Bibbins

Bo McGuire

Stephanie Heit

Petra Kuppers

Shannon Ivey

Sarah Bernhardt

Christina Nguyen Hung

Alice Wong

Mama Cax

Amy Monaghan

Jonathan Beecher Field

Lesley Jenike

Kaitlin Thomas

Danielle Pafunda

Seeley Quest

Ellen McGrath Smith

Karrie Higgins and

Ginna Raymer.

Have I ever met Kim Deal? No. Have I ever read her memoir? No. Am I completely unqualified to host this party? Yes. Why am I hosting this party?
FOR THE FUN OF IT.

Does anyone know where she is these days?

She's in my heart.

What is your favorite Kim Deal song?

So many good ones but maybe "Gigantic" takes the cake?

Oh man. The Breeders.

Which is your favorite song?!?

Laura Minor. So glad you're here!

I almost walked off tour once because my bass player wouldn't stop talking misogynistic trash about her. Agree to disagree? No. Take it back or I'm out.

Ooh. A party. I've always wondered why she went by Mrs. John Murphy?

Listening to the last Breeders album now. It's pretty good.

I haven't heard it yet. *All Nerve*, that one?

How does one attend this party?
You are here. So you're attending.

Did anyone ever make out to Kim Deal music?
I do not think I ever did. Please spill the details.

My junior high girlfriend, who was a few years older, gave
me *Come On Pilgrim* on cassette tape as a present.
That was a cool cassette because it had the whole album
on both sides.

I'll need someone to hold my mocktail. Going to event
and be back.

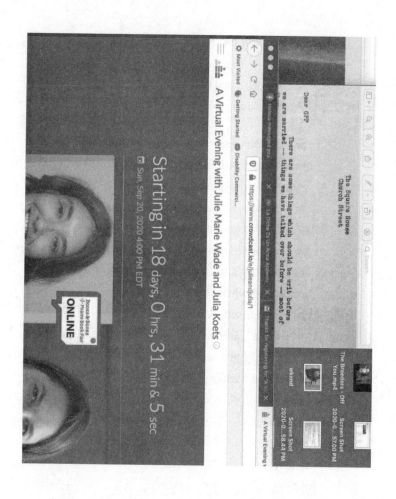

Starting in 18 days, 0 hrs, 31 min & 5 sec

📅 Sun, Sep 20, 2020 4:00 PM EDT

A Virtual Evening with Julie Marie Wade and Julia Koets ☺

WEBSITE FOR A KIM DEAL PARTY

Come in. John. Did you meet him. I did and I believed in him. Did you go away. No, I stayed a long time:

- ☐ I am a disabled person.
- ☐ I am a person with a disability.
- ☐ I am a person with a race.
- ☐ I am a person with a gender.
- ☐ I am a person with a sexuality.
- ☐ I am a cyborg in lineage with Hephaestus.
- ☐ I am a tryborg and I do not know it.
- ☐ I am ticking off the boxes.
- ☐ I am so confused. Who are you.
- ☐ I am Donna Haraway here to confiscate my good name.
- ☐ I am in pain right now.
- ☐ I am careful with my adverbs.
- ☐ And yours.
- ☐ My pronouns.
- ☐ And yours.
- ☐ My love.
- ☐ And yours.
- ☐ All the time.

Come in. John. Did you meet him. I did and I believed in him.
Did you go away. No, I stayed a long time:

> If a lasting link exists to A Kim Deal Party that I
> could watch, I would be so happy if you told me the
> details. I use a powerchair and psych meds and vast
> quantities of tea to get through my days.

I am a disabled person.

I am a person with a race.

I am ticking off the boxes.

I am in pain right now.

I am careful with my adverbs.

And yours.

My pronouns.

And yours.

My love.

And yours.

All the time.

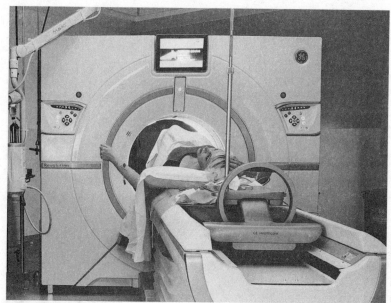

(Mistress Snow)

I am so confused. Who are you.
I am a cyborg in lineage with Hephaestus.
I am in pain right now.
And yours.

And yours.
And yours.
And yours.
All the time.

I am in pain right now.
My love.
All the time.

Hi Dylan,

Cy's assistant here, Amy (she/they). Attached is the design we want on the front of the shirts, toward the top of the shirt, right across the chest. Obviously, we don't want all the white space around the text, so y'all can just crop that out. Cy will likely follow up with another small logo/signature to print elsewhere on the shirts.

When Cy and I become Andy Warhol, we will thank you and Tonic for yr hard work.

x

ag

Hi Dylan,

So thrilled you're cool with the fast turnaround. As per color of shirts: I wish I knew Kim Deal's favorite color. By any chance, do you know it?

Cy

How about a game? We have reached the point in the party when _____.

We have reached the point in the party when an important fixture has been broken and I'm repairing it quietly so the party can continue.

We have reached the point in the party when we are texting people at other parties to tell them they should be at this one.

We have reached the point in the party when some new couple has very obviously disappeared.

Someone just said privately to me, "I have no idea who Kim Deal is," and THAT IS OKAY MY FRIEND YOU R STILL INVITED.

ACKNOWLEDGMENTS

My gratitude to the editors of these magazines where the poems first appeared:

Barrow Street: "All the Littles in Exodus"

Columbia: "Are There Any Lesbians Left in the Garden"

Crazyhorse: "Dream About the War on Opioids . . . ," "Sappho Fragment 51, Cyborg Version," "Klonopin, Come Back," and "What Is a Video Play"

Dodge Poetry Festival: "Ransom Note to the Dodge Poetry Festival . . ." and "Fountain by Marcel Duchamp"

Dreginald: "Ambien Poem"

Just Femme & Dandy: "Emo as I Dye My Hair"

Konch: "Poetry Entrance Exam"

Poetry: "DMs with Corbett O'Toole," "My Friend Says I Should Be Thinking About 'Masked Intimacy' When I Think of Leila Olive," "Color Study in Blue," "Romantic Gesture," "The Origins of Love," and "Sujet Supposé Savoir"

Poetry Is Currency: "Ambien Poem II"

The Rialto: "A Very Kind Note to Some Poets"

Some poems appeared in *Give It to Alfie Tonight*, a limited edition chapbook published by Red Mare Press.

For more on the video sonnets, check out Aga Skrodzka's essay "Strawberry Bondage and Disabling Discipline."

"A Kim Deal Party" is by invite only. You bought the book, so you are invited:

www.commoncyborg.com/AKimDealParty.

Access notes for the party: www.commoncyborg.com/AKDPNotes.

I'm incredibly grateful to everyone in "A Kim Deal Party." I'm grateful to Leela Chaitoo for signing this party. I'm grateful to John Loeppky for captioning it. I'm grateful to Suzannah Sinclair and Kelsey Scheaffer for advising on early iterations. I'm grateful to Amy Gaeta for believing in the party and to Sommer Browning for saying, "Put the party in the book." I'm grateful to my agent, Julia Kenny; my editor, Rachel Sargent; and the whole team at Ecco. I'm grateful to disabled elders who paved the way for me to imagine cyborg poems, video sonnets, and video plays. My love to Josh Bell.